All Sorts of Poems

Edited by Ann Thwaite

Illustrated by Patricia Mullins

D1392692

A Magnet Book

First published in Great Britain 1978
by Angus & Robertson (UK) Ltd
10 Earlham Street, London WC2H 9LP
Magnet edition first published 1980
by Methuen Children's Books Ltd,
11 New Fetter Lane, London EC4P 4EE
Reprinted 1982
This selection copyright © 1978 Ann Thwaite
Illustrations copyright © 1978 Angus & Robertson (UK) Ltd
Cover artwork copyright © 1980 Methuen Children's Books Ltd
Printed in Great Britain by
Richard Clay (The Chaucer Press) Ltd,
Bungay, Suffolk

ISBN 0 416 89570 0

Contents

Introduction

Most of the poems in this collection were first published in *Allsorts*, the annual collections of original stories, poems, articles, puzzles and so on I edited between 1968 and 1976. Many of them were written specially for *Allsorts* by well-known poets who rarely write for the young. Very few of these poems have been included in previous anthologies. And very few anthologies contain so many poems accessible to young children.

To the *Allsorts* poems I have added some others I particularly like. With hardly an exception, these poems have also been written during the past ten years.

The book is divided into sections. But these sections should not be taken too seriously. There is plenty of nonsense outside the 'Stuff and nonsense' section and there are plenty of people outside 'Some people'.

These poems remind children of the strangeness and richness of life and of language—and that poetry is not concerned only with daffodils and the moon and 'faery lands forlorn', but also with supermarkets and cinnamon buns, jigsaw puzzles and maths' tables.

ANN THWAITE

Advice to children

Advice to children

Caterpillars living on lettuce
Are the colour of their host:
Look out, when you're eating a salad,
For the greens that move the most.

Close your mouth tight when you're running
As when washing you shut your eyes,
Then as soap is kept from smarting
So will tonsils be from flies.

If in spite of such precautions
Anything nasty gets within,
Remember it will be thinking:
'Far worse for me than him.'

If in the middle of the night
Your bedside water tastes of cloth,
It means that possibly you might
By accident have drunk a moth.

In summer it's as well you should
Switch on the light before you sip,
For others actually could
Be taking then their midnight dip.

Plate-glass doors form a dangerous duo:
Never, when using them, try
To enter the place by the one marked TUO
Or withdraw through the one marked NI.

The world is dark with rumours
And things may happen to you.
Keep your handkerchief in your bloomers
And your money in your shoe.

ROY FULLER

The art of the possible

Ask for bunnies' ears—Notice on ice-cream van

Don't ask for automatic gears
Or Worthington's or Bass's beers
Or Scarborough or Brighton piers
Or three or even fewer cheers.

Don't ask for bandits' bandoliers
Or caliphs and their fat viziers;
Gazebos, ha-has, belvederes,
Or rapids, waterfalls and weirs.

Don't ask for eminent careers
Or universal panaceas.
Don't ask for alligators' tears
But, as you're told, for bunnies' ears.

ROY FULLER

How to open . . .

. . . Sardines

You don't have to grope in a
Drawer for an opener:
Sardines have a key and a lock.
There's an horrible slit
That you fit on a lip
And you turn like you're winding a clock.

It's blunt and it's bendable,
Thin and expendable,
Useless except for sardines.
You can easily lose it,
(And just try to use it
On cylinder-shaped tins of beans!)

It functions for feasting
Just once (like a bee-sting)
And doesn't grow rust in a drawer.
It curls up with the tin
Till it's stuck fast within,
And can't ever be used any more.

. . . Jam

You need a penny or a pin,
    And a pinch for the paper keeping the pips in.

. . . Coffee

                Twist
                    and
        ribbon   the
     tin   fragrance
      cut   gasps
      the   Strip
          off

... Baked beans

The tin-opener is a handleable sort of rhinoceros,
Snubandbumbling,butsharpasapairofbinoculars.
It is by the kind use of his snout
That the beans come shlurping out.

JOHN FULLER

13

When I was your age

When I was your age, child—
When I was eight,
When I was ten,
When I was two
(How old are you?)—
When I was your age, child,
My father would have gone quite *wild*
Had I behaved the way you
Do.
What, food uneaten on my plate
When I was eight?
What, room in such a filthy state
When I was ten?
What, late
For school when I was two?
My father would have shouted, 'When
I was your age, child, my father would have *raved*
Had I behaved
The way you
Do.'

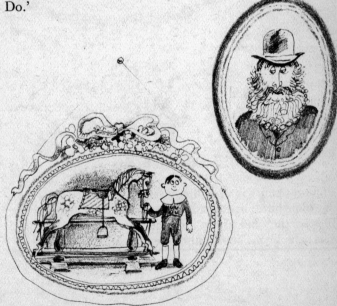

When I was
Your age, child, I did not drive us
All perpetually mad
By bashing
Up my little brother and reducing him to tears.
There was a war on in those years!
There were no brothers to be had!
Even sisters were on ration!
My goodness, we were pleased
To get *anything* to tease!
We were glad
Of aunts-and dogs,
Of chickens, grandmothers, and frogs;
Of creatures finned and creatures hooved,
And second cousins twice removed!

When I was your
Age, child, I was more
Considerate of others
(Particularly of fathers and of mothers).
I did not sprawl
Reading the *Dandy*
Or the *Beano*
When aunts and uncles came to call.
Indeed no.
I grandly
Entertained them all
With 'Please' and 'Thank you,' 'May I . . .?'
    'Thank you,' 'Sorry,' 'Please,'
And other remarks like these.
And if a chance came in the conversation
I would gracefully recite a line
Which everyone recognized as a quotation
From one of the higher multiplication
Tables, like 'Seven sevens are forty-nine.'

When I was your age, child, I
Should never have dreamed
Of sitting idly
Watching television half the night.
It would have seemed
Demented:
Television not then having been
Invented.

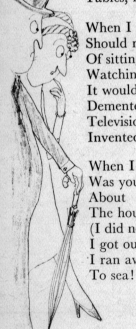

When I
Was your age, child, I did not lie
About
The house all day.
(I did not lie about anything at all—no liar I!)
I got out!
I ran away!
To sea!

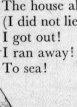

(Though naturally I was back, with hair brushed
   and hands washed, in time for tea.)
Oh yes, goodness me,
When I was nine
I had worked already down a diamond mine,
And fought in several minor wars,
And hunted boars
In the lonelier
Parts of Patagonia.
(Though I admit that possibly by then
I was getting on for ten.)
In the goldfields of Australia
I learned the bitterness of failure;
Experience in the temples of Siam
Made me the wise and punctual man I am;
But the lesson that I value most
I learned upon the Coromandel Coast—
Never, come what may, to boast.

When
I was your age, child, and the older generation
Offered now and then
A kindly explanation
Of what the world was like in their young day
I did not yawn in that rude way.
Why, goodness me,
There being no television to see
(As I have, I think, already said)
We were dashed grateful
For any entertainment we could get instead,
However tedious and hateful.

So grow up, child! And be
Your age! (What *is* your age, then?
Eight? Or nine? Or two? Or ten?)
Remember, as you look at me—
When I was your age I was forty-three.

MICHAEL FRAYN

Some people

Waking up Uncle

My uncle, General Doug MacDougal,
Sleeps nights inside a huge blue bugle
And when I'm feeling mean and devilly,
I blow him a bit of red-hot reveille.

He naps each noon. My favourite gag
Is filling Uncle's sleeping bag
With prune-whip yogurt to the brim.
It certainly surprises him
To jump in whistling happy tunes,
Then ooze back out, all gooey prunes.

He always chases me nine miles
And grabs me by the neck and smiles
And says, 'You've goofed again, you loafer —
Vanilla! That's the kind I go for!'

X. J. KENNEDY

Poor Nellie

There's a pitiful story — ah, me! —
Of a pretty young girl they called Nellie,
Who stared dumbly all day at TV
(If you want you can call it the 'telly').
She died young, and the reason, you see —
Her brains were all turned into jelly!

WILLIAM COLE

Simple Stan
Simple Stan was *mad* on fishes;
He'd catch them with a safety pin,
Then he'd kiss them, shout 'Best wishes!'
And gently toss them right back in!

WILLIAM COLE

21

Colonel Fazackerley

Colonel Fazackerley Butterworth-Toast
Bought an old castle complete with a ghost,
But someone or other forgot to declare
To Colonel Fazack that the spectre was there.

On the very first evening, while waiting to dine,
The Colonel was taking a fine sherry wine,
When the ghost, with a furious flash and a flare,
Shot out of the chimney and shivered, 'Beware!'

Colonel Fazackerley put down his glass
And said, 'My dear fellow, that's really first class!
I just can't conceive how you do it at all.
I imagine you're going to a Fancy Dress Ball?'

At this, the dread ghost gave a withering cry.
Said the Colonel (his monocle firm in his eye),
'Now just how you do it I wish I could think.
Do sit down and tell me, and please have a drink.'

The ghost in his phosphorous cloak gave a roar
And floated about between ceiling and floor.
He walked through a wall and returned through
    a pane
And backed up the chimney and came down again.

Said the Colonel, 'With laughter I'm feeling
    quite weak!'
(As trickles of merriment ran down his cheek.)
'My house-warming party I hope you won't spurn.
You must say you'll come and you'll give us a turn!'

At this, the poor spectre—quite out of his wits—
Proceeded to shake himself almost to bits.
He rattled his chains and he clattered his bones
And he filled the whole castle with mumbles
   and moans.

But Colonel Fazackerley, just as before,
Was simply delighted and called out, 'Encore!'
At which the ghost vanished, his efforts in vain,
And never was seen at the castle again.

'Oh dear, what a pity!' said Colonel Fazack.
'I don't know his name, so I can't call him back.'
And then with a smile that was hard to define,
Colonel Fazackerley went in to dine.

                    CHARLES CAUSLEY

Minstrel

The road unravels as I go,
walking into the sun, the anaemic
sun that lights Van Diemen's Land.
This week I have sung for my supper in seven towns.
I sleep in haysheds and corners
out of the wind, wrapped in a Wagga Rug.
In the mornings pools of mist fragment the country,
bits of field are visible higher up on ridges,
treetops appear, the mist hangs about for hours.
A drink at a valley river coming down
out of Mount Ossa; climb back to the road,
start walking, a song to warm these lips
whitebitten with cold.
In the hedges live tiny birds
who sing in bright colours you would not hear
from your fast vehicles. They sing for minstrels
and the sheep. The wires sing, too, with the wind;
also the leaves; it is not lonely.

MICHAEL DRANSFIELD

The boy at the end of our street

The boy at the end of our street gets everything.
He goes to town and never comes back
Without something to play with
Or something to wear.
I envy him.
He has no brothers or sisters to look after.
If you go to see if he is coming out to play,
He'll say:
   'We're playing at war only,
   And I am going to win.'

JOHN WILLIAMSON

24

Mrs McHingy

Old Mrs. McHingy so drab and so dingy,
Dressed all in black from her head to her toes,
She sits all alone in her old rocking chair
With her spectacles perched on her old beaky nose.
All by herself in her horrible kitchen
With no one to talk to, not even a cat.
But, 'Silence is golden,' says Mrs McHingy,
So nobody ever drops in for a chat.

Old Mrs McHingy so mean and so mingy
That strawberries and cream would just give her
   a pain,
She cooks onion soup in a steamy black pot
And sucks a strong peppermint now and again.
She doesn't get letters, or parcels or presents,
For birthdays she just wouldn't care in the least;
If you took her a cake with a hundred pink candles
She'd mumble, 'Enough is as good as a feast.'

Old Mrs McHingy so crabby and cringy,
Her slippers are worn and her clothes are in rags,
And she sits in her kitchen snipping and stitching
At oven cloths, aprons, and old duster bags.
She hasn't a thing that is perky and pretty,
She doesn't wear trinkets, or ribbons or rings.
'Waste not, and want not,' says Mrs McHingy,
'I never did hold with such frivolous things.'

Mrs McHingy so stuffy and stingy,
Oh, Mrs McHingy you'd better watch out,
For we're weaving a spell and we're making some
   'magic,
We'll dance on your doorstep and holler and shout:
'A hubble, a bubble, and abracadabra!'
And all of a sudden you'll jump from your chair;
You will skip to your window and let in the
   sunshine,
And take off your apron and curl up your hair.

You will tidy your kitchen so smoky and singy
And polish your mirror and powder your nose,
You will set your tea table with pretty blue china,
And dress yourself up in the gayest of clothes.
With a pink parasol, and a hat made of roses,
And little red shoes on your twinkling feet
You will run to your gate, and, 'Good morning,
   good morning,'
You'll call to the people who pass in the street.

'Good morning, good morning, it's lovely to see you.
Oh, won't you come in for a moment or two?
The kettle is on and the tea is all ready
With cream cakes and crumpets made specially
    for you.'
A yellow canary will sing at your window,
And people will come to your kitchen to see
Your gay chintzy curtains and scarlet geraniums,
And smile as you chatter and pass round the tea
In your beautiful gown all so flouncy and fringy,
'Delighted to know you, dear Mrs McHingy.'

DIANA HARLAND

Snow and so on

Snow

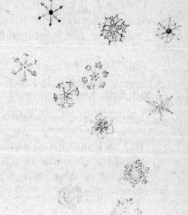

Snow falling in November
May fall on a yellow rose,
Forming an ice-cream cornet
That with ice-cream overflows.

When snow falls in December
It has only a bare black twig
To chalk on a sky of yellow
And make unusually big.

If snow should fall in April
How hard to tell its crumb
From petals cast in the border
Or blossom on the plum.

ROY FULLER

The weather

What's the weather on about?
Why is the rain so down on us?
Why does the sun glare at us so?

Why does the hail dance so prettily?
Why is the snow such an overall?
Why is the wind such a tearaway?

Why is the mud so fond of our feet?
Why is the ice so keen to upset us?
Who does the weather think it is?

GAVIN EWART

At nine of the night I opened my door

At nine of the night I opened my door
That stands midway between moor and moor,
And all around me, silver-bright,
I saw that the world had turned to white.

Thick was the snow on field and hedge
And vanished was the river-sedge,
Where winter skilfully had wound
A shining scarf without a sound.

And as I stood and gazed my fill
A stable-boy came down the hill.
With every step I saw him take
Flew at his heel a puff of flake.

His brow was whiter than the hoar,
A beard of freshest snow he wore,
And round about him, snow-flake starred,
A red horse-blanket from the yard.

In a red cloak I saw him go,
His back was bent, his step was slow,
And as he laboured through the cold
He seemed a hundred winters old.

I stood and watched the snowy head,
The whiskers white, the cloak of red.
'A Merry Christmas!' I heard him cry.
'The same to you, old friend,' said I.

CHARLES CAUSLEY

No knees and no nose

The rain has no knees
The snow has no nose
And so I suppose
The rain cannot graze
Its nothings of knees
And the snow when it froze
Couldn't sniff with a nose
All the smells that arose
From a pigsty or rose
And nobody sees
The noseless snow freeze
On shivery days
And nobody knows
How the rain ever goes
Soaking everyone's toes
Without walking with knees
But falls through the trees
Out of thundery skies
And falls on the seas
Without knowing the size
Of the squashy wet shoes
It would have if its toes
Were attached to some knees
And when the rain freezes
The snow which it causes
Has no knees *and* no nose
Because of the laws
That everyone knows
Which say 'Rain has no knees'
And 'Snow has no nose'.

But do you suppose
The rain cares about those
Laws with their clauses
Concerning no knees,
Or the snow ever pays
Attention to pleas
From a pig or a rose
For a nice snowy nose?

No, never. A sneeze
Wouldn't help when it snows
And as far as no knees goes
The rain goes its ways
Wherever it pleases
Untroubled by kneeses.

So there's no special cause
To make new decrees
To alter the laws
That the rain has no knees
And the snow has no nose.

ANTHONY THWAITE

Snowflake souffle

Snowflake souffle,
Snowflake souffle
Makes a lip-smacking lunch
On an ice-cold day.

You take seven snowflakes,
You break seven eggs,
And you stir it seven times
With your two hind legs.

Bake it in an igloo,
Throw it on a plate,
And slice off a slice
With a rusty ice-skate.

X. J. KENNEDY

Death of a snowman

I was awake all night,
Big as a polar bear,
Strong and firm and white.
The tall black hat I wear
Was draped with ermine fur.
I felt so fit and well
Till the world began to stir
And the morning sun swell.
I was tired, began to yawn;
At noon in the humming sun
I caught a severe warm;
My nose began to run.
My hat grew black and fell,
Was followed by my grey head.
There was no funeral bell,
But by tea-time I was dead.

VERNON SCANNELL

Rain

The lights are all on, though it's just past midday,
There are no more indoor games we can play,
No one can think of anything to say,
It rained all yesterday, it's raining today,
It's grey outside, inside me it's grey.

I stare out of the window, fist under my chin,
The gutter leaks drips on the lid of the dustbin,
When they say 'Cheer up', I manage a grin,
I draw a fish on the glass with a sail-sized fin,
It's sodden outside, and it's damp within.

Matches, bubbles and papers pour into the drains,
Clouds smother the sad laments from the trains,
Grandad says it brings on his rheumatic pains,
The moisture's got right inside of my brains,
It's raining outside, inside me it rains.

BRIAN LEE

37

Feathered friends

Late winter

The pallid cuckoo
Sent up in frail
Microtones
His rising scale
On the cold air.
What joy I found
Mounting that tiny
Stair of sound.

JAMES MCAULEY

After breakfast

I stop myself sliding a morsel
Of bacon fat into the bin.
It will do as a meal for the robin,
His legs are so terribly thin.

ROY FULLER

Night herons

It was after a day's rain:
the street facing the west
was lit with growing yellow;
the black road gleamed.

First one child looked and saw
and told another.
Face after face, the windows
flowered with eyes.

It was like a long fuse lighted,
the news travelling.
No one called out loudly;
everyone said 'Hush.'

The light deepened; the wet road
answered in daffodil colours,
and down its centre
walked the two tall herons.

Stranger than wild birds, even,
what happened on those faces:
suddenly believing in something,
they smiled and opened.

Children thought of fountains,
circuses, swans feeding:
women remembered words
spoken when they were young.

Everyone said 'Hush;'
no one spoke loudly;
but suddenly the herons
rose and were gone. The light faded.

JUDITH WRIGHT

Vulture

The vulture's very like a sack
Set down and left there drooping.
His crooked neck and creaky beak
Look badly bent from stooping
Down to the ground to eat dead cows
So they won't go to waste,
Thus making up in usefulness
For what he lacks in taste.

X. J. KENNEDY

One day at a Perranporth pet-shop

One day at a Perranporth pet-shop
On a rather wild morning in June,
A lady from Par bought a budgerigar
And she sang to a curious tune:
'Say that you love me, my sweetheart,
My darling, my dovey, my pride,
My very own jewel, my dear one!'
'Oh lumme,' the budgie replied.

'I'll feed you entirely on cream-cakes
And doughnuts all smothered in jam,
And puddings and pies of incredible size,
And peaches and melons and ham.
And you shall drink whiskies and sodas,
For comfort your cage shall be framed.
You shall sleep in a bed lined with satin.'
'Oh crikey!' the budgie exclaimed.

But the lady appeared not to hear him
For she showed neither sorrow nor rage,
As with common-sense tardy and action foolhardy
She opened the door of his cage.
'Come perch on my finger, my honey,
To show you are mine, O my sweet.' —
Whereupon the poor fowl with a shriek and a howl
Took off like a jet down the street.

And he flew up above **Cornwall**
To ensure his escape was no failure,
Then his speed he increased and he flew south
   and east
To his ancestral home in Australia.

For although to the Australian abo
The word 'budgerigar' means 'good food',
He said, 'I declare I'll feel much safer there
Than in Bodmin or Bugle or Bude.'

      Envoy
And I'm sure with the budgie's conclusion
You all will agree without fail:
Best eat frugal and free in a far-distant tree
Than down all the wrong diet in jail.

               CHARLES CAUSLEY

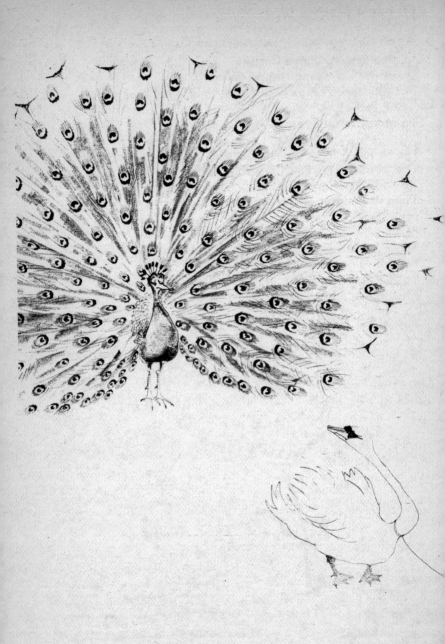

I'll buy a peacock bird

When I have a beard that's curly and weird,
I'll buy myself a peacock bird.
He'll shout, 'Hello, hello, hello,'
As on my lawns he'll to and fro.
Other birds will hop and glare
As he sheds feathers here and there.

I'll ask my Aunty Maud to tea
(For she has swans and a maple tree)
To view my peacock on my lawn
Who shouts 'Hello' from the break of dawn,
And spy his mantle spreading wide
All shimmering blue and golden-eyed.

MODWENA SEDGWICK

Creatures great and small

My tortoise

I had a sweet tortoise called Pye
Wabbit.
He ate dandelions, it was
His habit.
Pye Wabbit, Pye Wy-et,
It was more than a habit, it was
His diet.
All the hot summer days, Pye
Wy-et, Pye Wiked-it,
Ate dandelions. I lay on the grass flat to see
How much he liked it.
In the autumn when it got cold, Pye Wiked-it, Pye
Wy-bernator,
Went to sleep till next spring. He was
a hibernator.
First he made a secret bed for the winter,
To lie there.
We loved him far too much ever
To spy where.
Why does his second name change every time?
Why, to make the rhyme.
Pye our dear tortoise
Is dead and gone.
He lies in the tomb we built for him, called
'Pye's Home'.
Pye, our dear tortoise,
We loved him so much.
Is he as dear to you now
As he was to us?

STEVIE SMITH

Squirrel

Oh the elephant strolls, the turkey struts,
But the squirrel leaps from tree to tree.
He is lithe and swift, he is nuts on nuts
But he will not wait for me.

The blindworm slithers, the monkey swings,
But the squirrel flies like a bird.
When I begged him to teach me how
He pretended he hadn't heard.

Oh the pather pounces, the cheetah pads,
The lynx slinks, (the skunk stinks) and rabbits run.
But I wanted to leap like a squirrel
And before I could ask him he was gone.

JAMES FENTON

A fox came into my garden

A fox came into my garden.
'What do you want from me?'
'Heigh-ho, Johnnie-boy,
A chicken for my tea.'

'Oh no, you beggar, and never, you thief,
My chicken you must leave,
That she may run and she may fly
From now to Christmas Eve.'

'What are you eating, Johnnie-boy,
Between two slices of bread?'
'I'm eating a piece of chicken-breast
And it's honey-sweet,' I said.

'Heigh-ho, you diddling man,
I thought that was what I could smell.
What, some for you and none for me?
Give us a piece as well.'

CHARLES CAUSLEY

Animals are beasts

When looking for supper
Or catering for feasts
Men may be cruel
But animals are beasts.

JAMES FENTON

Sheep party

Under thorn and bramble
The sheep have left their rags
And decorate the valley
With little woollen flags.

This way to the party,
The wispy tufts declare.
Between the banks and hedges,
Hurry, you're nearly there!

There's bracken newly curling
And bilberry in bloom,
The guests are quite contented
And there's lots and lots of room.

But who am I to follow
And which way should I go?
The wool is blue and crimson
And from different sheep, I know.

The red-stained sheep live *that* way,
The blue-stained sheep up *there*.
There must be several parties
And I really couldn't care.

For I like peanut butter
Not grass and twigs and stones
Like the red sheep of Mr Roberts
And the blue of Mr Jones.

JOHN FULLER

Halfway

I saw a tadpole once in a sheet of ice
(a freakish joke played by my country's weather).
He hung at arrest, displayed as it were in glass,
an illustration of neither one thing nor the other.

His head was a frog's and his hinder legs had grown
ready to climb and jump to his promised land;
but his bladed tail in the ice-pane weighed him down.
He seemed to accost my eye with his budding hand.

'I am neither one thing nor the other, not here
    nor there.
I saw great lights in the place where I would be,
but rose too soon, half made for water, half air,
and they have gripped and stilled and enchanted me.

'Is that world real, or a dream I cannot reach?
Beneath me the dark familiar waters flow
and my fellows huddle and nuzzle each to each,
while motionless here I stare where I cannot go.'

The comic O of his mouth, his gold-rimmed eyes,
looked in that lustrous glaze as though they'd ask
my vague divinity, looming in stooped surprise,
for death or rescue. But neither was my task.

Waking halfway from a dream one winter night
I remembered him as a poem I had to write.

JUDITH WRIGHT

Better be kind to them now

A squirrel is digging up the bulbs
In half the time Dad took to bury them.

A small dog is playing football
With a mob of boys. He beats them all,
Scoring goals at both ends.
A kangaroo would kick the boys as well.

Birds are so smart they can drink milk
Without removing the bottle-top.

Cats stay clean, and never have to be
Carried screaming to the bathroom.
They don't get their heads stuck in railings,
They negotiate first with their whiskers.

The gecko walks on the ceiling, and
The cheetah can outrun the Royal Scot.
The lion cures his wounds by licking them,
And the guppy has fifty babies at a go.

The cicada plays the fiddle for hours on end,
And a man-size flea could jump over St Paul's.

If ever these beasts should get together
Then we are done for, children.
I don't much fancy myself as a python's pet,
But it might come to that.

D. J. ENRIGHT

Take one home for the kiddies

On shallow straw, in shadeless glass,
Huddled by empty bowls, they sleep:
No dark, no dam, no earth, no grass —
Mam, get us one of them to keep.

Living toys are something novel,
But it soon wears off somehow.
Fetch the shoebox, fetch the shovel —
Mam, we're playing funerals now.

PHILIP LARKIN

Small, smaller

I thought that I knew all there was to know
Of being small, until I saw once, black against
     the snow,
A shrew, trapped in my footprint, jump and fall
And jump again and fall, the hole too deep, the
     walls too tall.

RUSSELL HOBAN

Our doggy

First he sat, and then he lay,
And then he said: I've come to stay.
And that is how we acquired our doggy Pontz.
He is all right as dogs go, but not quite what one
     wants.
Because he talks. He talks like you and me.
And he is not you and me, he is made differently.
You think it is nice to have a talking animal?
It is not nice. It is unnatural.

STEVIE SMITH

Belinda and Jill

There once were two cows named Belinda and Jill
Who lived side by side on a very steep hill.
Jill was a Jersey of elegant grace,
And Belinda was brown with a square kind of face.
They lived very quiet and contented together
Admiring the view and wondering whether
The grass was more sweet to the east or the west,
Or whether the top of the hill was the best.
'What more could we wish,' said Belinda to Jill,
'Than to live side by side on this excellent hill?'
'I could ask for no more than a friend such as you,'
Replied Jill, as she blissfully gazed at the view.

Now they might have gone on in this amiable way
If it hadn't occurred that one bright summer's day
The farmer came by with his axe and a spade,
And a handful of nails, and a hammer, and made
A new gate through the hedge that they'd never
   seen over
That led to the field where he grew his best clover.

Now all cows are curious, you will agree,
And Jill and Belinda stood spellbound to see
In the very next field such a wonderful sight
As the buttercups golden, and clover so white.
'Oh dear,' sighed Belinda, 'I would like to taste

Just one handful of clover — it does seem a waste
To see it and smell it, and have it so near,
And never to taste it!' But Jill did not hear,
As she pictured herself looking dainty and sweet
With clover and buttercups spread at her feet.

So day after day they would stand by the gate,
And wonder and wonder and patiently wait,
Hoping the farmer would let them go through
To the field where the clover and buttercups grew.
And Belinda grew crosser and crosser until
She had hardly a moment to spare for poor Jill,
As she mumbled and grumbled and always
    looked grumpy;
'To live all your life on a hill that's so humpy,
And only have grass, and old hay from a stack —
I'm going away, and I'm not coming back!'
But Jill drifted on in a wonderful dream,
Till she really believed, and it really did seem,
That she lay in a clover and buttercup bed
With a wreath of white daisies adorning her head;
And she climbed up the hill in a beautiful trance
Without giving the gate or Belinda a glance.

Now if any evening you happen to go
By the field where the clover and buttercups grow,
You will see side by side on the top of the hill
Sulky Belinda and whimsical Jill;
And Jill will not look and Belinda won't speak,
Though the gate has been open for over a week.

DIANA HARLAND

Fat cat

Siamese have cobalt eyes, their tails are thin and
   kinky,
Siamese are slender, Siamese are slinky,
The experts are agreed on that —
They haven't seen this family cat.

His fur is sleek, his eyes are blue,
His pedigree is long and true —
But what a figure! What a weight!
And how he eats! At what a rate!
For pussy hasn't read the books,
He doesn't know how wrong he looks.

Left-over yogurt, frozen peas,
Spaghetti, any kind of cheese,
He wolfs them down (if that's the word)
Then ups and outs and grabs a bird.
He sits below the baby's chair
To catch the dropped bits in the air,
The phone rings and you turn your back,
He's on the table, snicker snack.

We tried to keep him slim and lean,
He got bad-tempered, scratchy, mean,
And used to tour the neighbours' bins
And leave the bits — fish bones and skins —
On our front doorstep. And one time
He stole their Sunday joint, a crime
We really felt must be prevented;
So now he's fat, full and contented,
The Siamese who over-ate,
Our greedy, gross, unusual pet.

MARY RAYNER

Death of a mouse

A mouse returning late one night
Happy, or mildly drunk,
Danced a gavotte by the pale moonlight.
An owl caught sight of him.
Clunk.

JAMES FENTON

Cows

The cows that browse in pastures
Seem not at all surprised
That as they moo they mow the lawn
And their milk comes pasture-ized.

X. J. KENNEDY

Who to pet and who not to

Go pet a kitten, pet a dog,
Go pet a worm for practice,
But don't go pet a porcupine —
You want to be a cactus?

X. J. KENNEDY

The dog

The dog is a traditional beast.
He is made to hunt and feast
And fight
And roll his lawless eyes at his fellows.
He attacks his enemies with slashing and dashing,
Stunning and running
Back to his lair
With his mouthful of hair.
The dog has a traditional appetite.
His gullet is made for guzzling lumps of
    unchewed food.
His stomach functions with grumblings and
    rumblings.
Like a baron he sprawls,
Sides heaving like bellows,
Shreds of meat in his jaws.
The dog, like the baron, is rustic and rude.
He relieves himself against walls
And the uprights of doors.
The dog and the baron fight the same wars,
Growl with the same throat,
Brothers under the coat.

PRUDENCE ANDREW

My yellow friend

When the lion roars in the jungle
The moisture shakes from the trees
And the swift invisible hummingbirds
Rustle in the scented breeze

And the slimey snakes slip silently
From the green sun-dappled grass
And the beasts retreat from the forest glade
To watch the lion pass.

I was tired and hot and cared not a jot
For prudence, wisdom or thrift:
When the lion came by, I cried out 'Hi!'
And asked it for a lift.

Now I know I can go anywhere that I care
With my yellow friend for a guide
But I always go back to the forest track
With the scented breeze from the banyan trees
And the sound of the lion's stride.

JAMES FENTON

My mother saw a dancing bear

My mother saw a dancing bear
By the schoolyard, a day in June.
The keeper stood with chain and bar
And whistle-pipe, and played a tune.

And bruin lifted up its head
And lifted up its dusty feet,
And all the children laughed to see
It caper in the summer heat.

They watched as for the Queen it died.
They watched it march. They watched it halt.
They heard the keeper as he cried,
'Now, roly-poly!' 'Somersault!'

And then, my mother said, there came
The keeper with a begging-cup,
The bear with burning coat of fur,
Shaming the laughter to a stop.

They paid a penny for the dance,
But what they saw was not the show;
Only, in bruin's aching eyes,
Far-distant forests, and the snow.

CHARLES CAUSLEY

Children talking

Fever dream

Tossed with fever on my bed,
I thought the clock might wake the dead;
At twelve it struck so mad a din,
I wondered, would it strike thirteen?
Before that came I counted sheep
And had a dream in troubled sleep:
I looked across the road at night
And saw a window filled with light;
And someone looking out of it,
Whose face was in the shade, unlit,
Seemed to be looking back at me:
It was a face I had to see.
I tried and tried to pierce the shade,
And suddenly became afraid:
A light came on, and I could name
That person in the window frame:
His features scared me to the bone:
I looked again — they were my own.

EDWARD LOWBURY

Late for breakfast

Who is it hides my sandals when I'm trying to get
   dressed?
And takes away the hairbrush that was lying on
   the chest?
I wanted to start breakfast before any of the others
But something's always missing or been
   borrowed by my brothers.
I think I'd better dress at night, and eat my
   breakfast too,
      Then when everybody's hurrying —
      I'll have nothing else to do.

MARY DAWSON

Supermarket

I'm
lost
among a
maze of cans,
behind a pyramid
of jams, quite near
asparagus and rice,
close to the Oriental spice,
and just before sardines.
I hear my mother calling, 'Joe.
Where are you, Joe? Where did you
Go?' And I reply in a voice concealed among
the candied orange peel, and packs of Chocolate
Dreams.

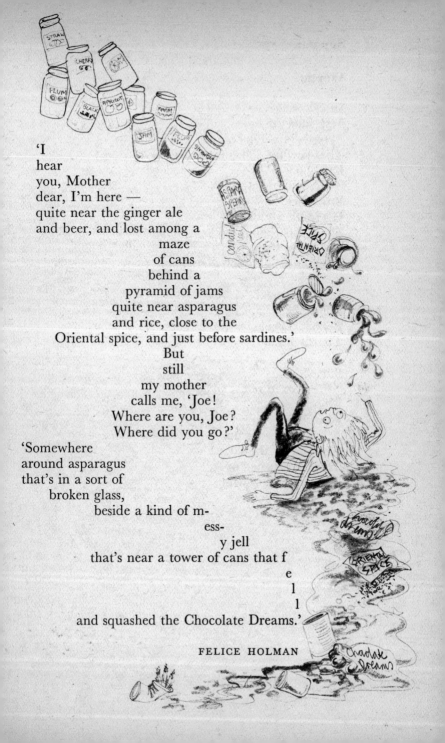

'I
hear
you, Mother
dear, I'm here —
quite near the ginger ale
and beer, and lost among a
maze
of cans
behind a
pyramid of jams
quite near asparagus
and rice, close to the
Oriental spice, and just before sardines.'
But
still
my mother
calls me, 'Joe!
Where are you, Joe?
Where did you go?'

'Somewhere
around asparagus
that's in a sort of
broken glass,
beside a kind of m-
ess-
y jell
that's near a tower of cans that f
e
l
l
and squashed the Chocolate Dreams.'

FELICE HOLMAN

Words

Sticks and stones
May break my bones
But words can never hurt me —
That is what I'm supposed to say.
But:
'One, two, three,
Brian Lee —
His mother picks his fleas,
She roasts them,
She toasts them,
They have them for their teas.'

Sticks and stones
May break my bones
But words can never hurt me —
That is what I say.

But:
'One, two, three,
Bri-an Lee
Went to sea,
A big fish swam up
Got him by the knee.
The boat turned over,
Brian couldn't swim.
I wonder whatever
Happened to him.'

Sticks and stones
May break my bones
But . . . .

'One, two, three,
Bri-an Lee
Went for a pee —
Never came back.
Found him later,
Put him in a sack.'

Sticks and stones . . . .
But . . . .
Words can prick,
Can pierce, can sting,
Can cut, can stab,
Can scar, can sling.
This is what I shout back:

'George Rudden
Is fat as a pig,
He eats so much pudden
His belly gets big.'

'Mary McVicker's
Brain's gone numb,
When she bends over
We can all see her bum.
She's forgot to put them on —
No-knickers
Mary McVickers.'

'Freddie Bell
's got feet that smell —
He won't change his socks.
Shut him in a cell,
Drop him down a well,
Nail him in a box.'

But . . . .
They won't clear off.
Nothing I say
Seems quite good enough
To hurt them as much
As they hurt me . . . .
Though I stand and shout
Till some mister comes out
And tells me to go away.

Sticks and stones
May break my bones —

With a pound of plaster
Your bones get better —
But once it's been heard,
Who forgets the Word?

BRIAN LEE

Bringing up babies

If babies could speak they'd tell mother or nurse
That slapping was pointless, and why:
For if you're not crying it prompts you to cry,
And if you are — then you cry worse.

ROY FULLER

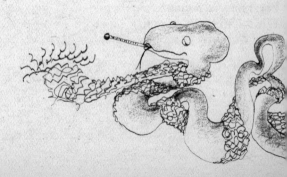

The useful art of knitting

When Mum sits down to knit at night
Her patterns seem to go just right.
She doesn't even have to look;
She can knit and read a book.
But, oh, the worry
And the flurry
When I sit
And try to knit!
My stitches always get too tight
Or else I drop them out of sight.
I split the wool and big holes come,
I pass my knitting back to Mum.
I grizzle and I grumble,
I struggle and I mumble.
I feel just like that girl Matilda
('The effort very nearly killed her.')
Mum says, 'Don't worry, try once more.'
I throw my knitting on the floor.
We both get cross; I go to bed
And a wonderful dream comes into my head:
When my knitting is finished
I shall win First Prize
for
The Most Original
Best Ventilated
Multi-coloured
Complicated
Scarf
Knitted by a Demented Spider
For an Oddly-shaped Snake
With a Very
Sore Throat.

KATHERINE CRAIG

Intelligence test

'What do you use your eyes for?'
The white-coated man enquired.
'I use my eyes for looking,'
Said Toby, ' — unless I'm tired.'

'I see. And then you close them,'
Observed the white-coated man.
'Well done. A very good answer.
Let's try another one.

'What is your nose designed for?
What use is the thing to you?'
'I use my nose for smelling,'
Said Toby, 'don't you, too?'

'I do indeed,' said the expert,
'That's what the thing is for.
Now I've another question to ask you,
Then there won't be any more.

'What are your ears intended for?
Those things at each side of your head?
Come on — don't be shy — I'm sure you can say.'
'For washing behind,' Toby said.

VERNON SCANNELL

The radio men

When I was little more than six
I thought that men must be
Alive inside the radio
To act in plays, or simply blow
Trumpets, or sing to me.

I never got a glimpse of them,
They were so very small.
But I imagined them in there,
Their voices bursting on the air
Through that thin, wooden wall.

ELIZABETH JENNINGS

What shall I do?

The wind pulls the smoke from the chimney-pots
Into the cold thin rain.
Over the road a dog sidles, sniffs, trots
By the boards that shut off the weedy lots
And turns up the lane:
No one will call this afternoon.
What shall I do now, Mummy?
What shall I do?

My finger squeaks in the steam on the pane —
A house, a face, a boat.
One sweep of my sleeve and they are gone;
My vest and socks drip on to the lawn,
There's no one about.
Don't want to stay in, or go out.
What shall I do now, Mummy?
What shall I do?

Books, comics and marbles, my clockwork train,
Puzzles I've done before,
Cards and dominoes, a pistol and plane,
Tin soldiers, cars, a meccano crane
All over the floor:
There's nothing to play with there.
What shall I do now, Mummy?
What shall I do?

I see time pass in the glass-sided clock
Ticking above the fire,
But the hands hardly move, though I turn my back,
Two minutes have gone since I last turned to look,
It seems like an hour . . .
Seems like a month . . . like a year. . . .
What shall I do now, Mummy?
What shall I do?

What time is tea? Can I have something to eat?
When will Daddy get back?
What are you doing? Can I have one more sweet?
Where does the bus go from the end of the street?
How long does it take?
What do you mean — 'For goodness' sake?'
What shall I do now, Mummy?
What shall I do?

One sweep of my hand can wipe it all out,
One blow could knock down
The domino skyscraper, the wood-block fort,
The castle of cards, and the crane; one shout
Upset everyone,
Make them all ask what's wrong. But then?
What shall I do now, Mummy?
What shall I do?

BRIAN LEE

A house without children

A house without children
is like a tree without birds
says the old proverb.

The house was full of birds—
budgerigars, canaries
goldfinches—a dazzling
deafening family

raised by my aunt and uncle.
I went to stay with them
one summer holiday.

And they said a footprint
here and there, the odd chatter
was all right: but not, please not
mud and screeches all the time.

Why couldn't I be like
the birds in their cages?
And they sent me home.

I didn't mind. A house
with so many birds
is like a tree you've climbed
and can't get down.

KEITH BOSLEY

They're calling

They're calling, 'Nan,
Come at once.'
But I don't answer.
       It's not that I don't hear,
       I'm very sharp of ear,
But I'm not Nan,
I'm a dancer.

They're calling, 'Nan,
Go and wash.'
But I don't go yet.
   Their voices are quite clear,
   I'm humming but I hear,
But I'm not Nan,
I'm a poet.

They're calling, 'Nan,
Come to dinner!'
And I stop humming.
   I seem to hear them clearer,
   Now that dinner's nearer.
Well, just for now I'm Nan,
And I say, 'Coming.'

FELICE HOLMAN

The jigsaw puzzle

My beautiful picture of pirates and treasure
Is spoiled, and almost I don't want to start
To put it together; I've lost all the pleasure
I used to find in it: there's one missing part.

I know there's one missing—they lost it, the others,
The last time they played with my puzzle —
 and maybe
There's more than one missing: along with the
 brothers
And sisters who borrow my toys there's the baby.

There's a hole in the ship or the sea that it sails on,
And I said to my father, 'Well, what shall I do?,
It isn't the same now that some of it's gone.'
He said, 'Put it together; the world's like that too.'

RUSSELL HOBAN

Cold feet

They have all gone across
They are all turning to see
They are all shouting 'Come on'
They are all waiting for me.

I look through the gaps in the footway
And my heart shrivels with fear,
For way below the river is flowing
So quick and so cold and so clear.

And all that there is between it
And me falling down there is this:
A few wooden planks (not very thick)
And between each, a little abyss.

The holes get right under my sandals,
I can see straight through to the rocks,
And if I don't look, I can feel it,
Just there, through my shoes and my socks.

Suppose my feet and my legs withered up
And slipped through the slats like a rug?
Suppose I suddenly went very thin
Like the baby that slid down the plug?

I know that it cannot happen
But suppose that it did, what then?
Would they be able to find me
And take me back home again?

They have all gone across
They are all waiting to see
They are all shouting 'Come on' —
But they'll have to carry me.

BRIAN LEE

Strange stories

Mother, a dog is at the door

Mother, a dog is at the door
Demanding your moleskin hat.
No, daughter my child, it drives dogs wild,
We don't dare give him that.

Mother, he said he'd take instead
Your billygoat's old canoe.
Good gracious, no! That isn't to go.
It's stuck fast with airplane glue.

Mother, he'd trade some lemonade
For your bicycle-pumpkin pie.
Oh, would he, the bum? If I lost one crumb
Of that delicate stuff I'd die!

Mother, I'm scared. He's all bristly-haired!
He's foaming like canned whipped-cream!
Tell him, my dear, that indeed I fear
I shall stand on my head and scream.

Oh, mother, he's peeling his teeth away —
It's Father in dog's disguise.
Why, daughter my own, I ought to have known
That a dog wouldn't want my pies.

X. J. KENNEDY

Tom's bomb

There was a boy whose name was Tom,
Who made a high explosive bomb,
By mixing up some iodine
With sugar, flour and plasticine.
Then, to make it smell more queer,
He added Daddy's home-made beer.
He took it off to school one day,
And when they all went out to play,
He left it by the radiator.
As the heat was getting greater,
The mixture in the bomb grew thick
And very soon it seemed to tick.
Miss Knight came in and gazed with awe
To see the bomb upon the floor.
'Dear me,' she said, 'it is a bomb,
An object worth escaping from.'
She went to Mr Holliday
And said in tones that were not gay,
'Headmaster, this is not much fun;
There is a bomb in Classroom One.'
'Great snakes,' said he, and gave a cough
And said, 'I hope it won't go off.
But on the off-chance that it does,
I think we'd better call the fuzz.'
A policeman came and said, 'Oh God,
We need the bomb disposal squad,
Some firemen and a doctor too,

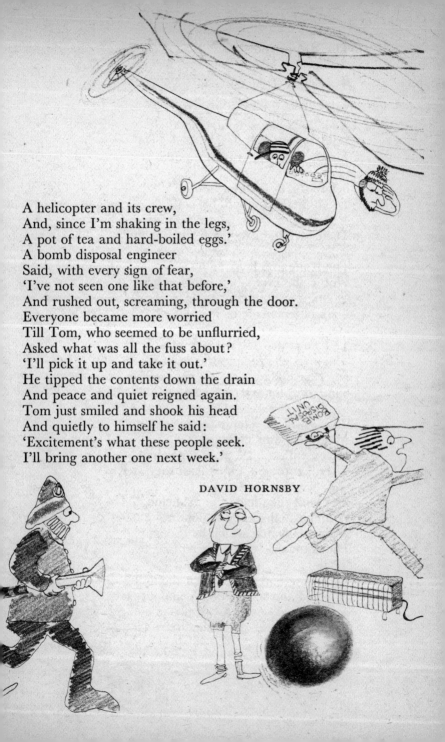

A helicopter and its crew,
And, since I'm shaking in the legs,
A pot of tea and hard-boiled eggs.'
A bomb disposal engineer
Said, with every sign of fear,
'I've not seen one like that before,'
And rushed out, screaming, through the door.
Everyone became more worried
Till Tom, who seemed to be unflurried,
Asked what was all the fuss about?
'I'll pick it up and take it out.'
He tipped the contents down the drain
And peace and quiet reigned again.
Tom just smiled and shook his head
And quietly to himself he said:
'Excitement's what these people seek.
I'll bring another one next week.'

DAVID HORNSBY

The Kangaroo's coff

*A Poem for Children Ill in Bed, Indicating to Them
the Oddities of our English Orthography*

The eminent Professor Hoff
Kept, as a pet, a Kangaroo
Who, one March day, started a coff
That very soon turned into floo.

Before the flu carried him off
To hospital (still with his coff),
A messenger came panting through
The door, and saw the Kangarough.

The Kangaroo lay wanly there
Within the Prof's best big armchere,
Taking (without the power to chew)
A sip of lemonade or tew.

'O Kangaroo,' the fellow said,
'I'm glad you're not already daid,
For I have here (pray do not scoff)
Some stuff for your infernal coff.

'If you will take these powdered fleas,
And just a tiny lemon squeas
Mixed with a little plain tapwater,
They'll cure you. Or at least they ater.'

Prof Hoff then fixed the medicine,
Putting the fleas and lemon ine
A glass of water, which he brought
The Kangaroo as he'd been tought.

The Kangaroo drank down the draught,
Shivered and scowled — then oddly laught
And vaulted out of the armchair
Before the Prof's astonished stair —

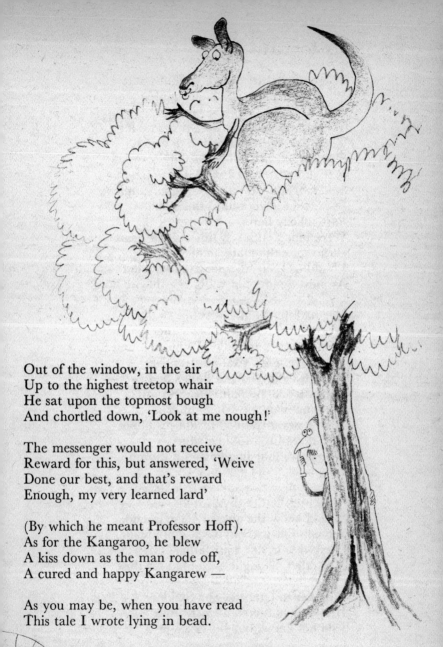

Out of the window, in the air
Up to the highest treetop whair
He sat upon the topmost bough
And chortled down, 'Look at me nough!'

The messenger would not receive
Reward for this, but answered, 'Weive
Done our best, and that's reward
Enough, my very learned lard'

(By which he meant Professor Hoff).
As for the Kangaroo, he blew
A kiss down as the man rode off,
A cured and happy Kangarew —

As you may be, when you have read
This tale I wrote lying in bead.

ANTHONY THWAITE

Stables' tables

There was a girl called Sheila Stables
Who never really knew her tables.
At least, with study she was able
To get to know the twice times table;
Then having had revealed the trick,
She learned her ten times fairly quick.
A friend of hers called Mabel Gimpel
Said five and eleven were just as simple,
But Sheila never found this so.
Particularly hard to know
Were nine and seven times. Miss Bass
(Who took the mathematics class)
Would call out: 'Sheila Stables, what
Are seven nines? . . . Oh, no, they're not.'

Her bad marks in this subject rather
Worried her. She told her father,
Who laughed and said: 'Why goodness me,
There are more vital matters, She,
Than learning boring things by heart —
For instance, human love, and art.'
A poetic man was Mr Stables
Who'd never quite got right his tables
And if required to do a sum
Would use four fingers and a thumb.

'What's nine times seven?' asked Miss Bass.
'Only, my father says, an ass
Would know the answer,' Sheila said,
Though not without a sense of dread.
'I asked you, not your father,' Miss
Bass cried. 'Nought out of ten for this.'

Whether in later life She Stables
Had ever mastered all her tables
I do not know, but she became

A greater player of the game
Than even the formidable Bass.
She worked out when the sun would pass
Behind the planet Minotaur
(A body quite unknown before
The book of astronomic tables
Compiled by Dr Sheila Stables);
And put, the right way up, a bit
Of puzzle Einstein failed to fit.

It seemed the world did not depend
On having at one's fingers' end
Nine eights or seven sixes — though
Poetry itself could never show
(As Sheila was the first to say)

The Past, the Purpose and the Way:
Somewhere among the curious laws
Enacted by the Primal Cause
There enters (usually in the heavens)
Such things as nine, or seven, sevens.

ROY FULLER

The headless gardener

A gardener, Tobias Baird,
sent his head to be repaired;
he thought, as nothing much was wrong,
he wouldn't be without it long.

Ten years he's weeded path and plot,
a headless gardener, God wot,
always hoping (hope is vain)
To see his noddle back again.
Don't pity him for his distress —
he never sent up his address.

IAN SERRAILLIER

Horace's Christmas Disappointment

Young Horace Giraffe on Christmas Eve
Put out his stocking to receive
Whatever Santa Claus might bring.
You may indeed be wondering
What sort of size such stockings are,
Since even small giraffes are far
Bigger than quite a tall man is.
Young Horace Giraffe had measured his,
And found it stretched four feet or so
From ample top to roomy toe.

What piles and piles of presents he
Imagined packed there presently!
A hundred tangerines; a bunch
Of ripe bananas for his lunch;
Five watermelons; fifty figs;
The most delicious juicy sprigs

Plucked from the tops of special trees
With leaves as sweet as honey-bees;
And in the very bottom, some
Chocolates full of candied rum.

Alas, poor Horace! Christmas Day
Dawned, and he rose from where he lay
To snatch the stocking from the bed —
But though it bulged, he felt with dread
How light it was . . . He reached inside —
And then he very nearly died.

Inside the stocking, almost half
The size of Horace, was a SCARF
(A useful garment, yes, I know,
But oh it was a bitter blow.)
The scarf was fully ten yards long,
And striped and bright and very strong.
It filled the stocking, top to toe,
And Horace was quite filled with woe.

The moral is: A *USEFUL* PRESENT
    IN STOCKINGS IS RATHER
        SELDOM PLEASANT

ANTHONY THWAITE

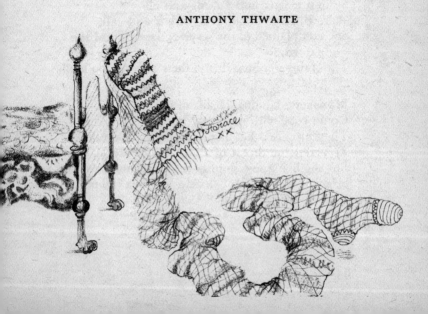

Aunt Kate: a moral story

When Aunt Kate woke each shining day
She started nagging right away.
'Shut the window,' 'Open the door,'
'Pick your pyjamas up from the floor,'
'Let the cat in,' 'Make some tea,'
'Why do you never listen to me?'
'Stop fidgeting,' 'Your tie is bent.'
She started so and on it went
From breakfast through to supper-time,
Till even breathing seemed a crime.
Her nephews and her nieces too
Were at their wits' ends what to do.

One summer-time she made a plan
To spend a week with Cousin Anne.
She turned the gas off, packed her case,
Left her instructions all over the place.
She went to the station to catch her train,
And her nieces began to smile again.
Her nephews started to laugh and sing
And they wouldn't be quiet for anything.
Meanwhile at the station, Aunt Kate found
A way to boss everyone around;
Station master and guards and all
Were running about at her beck and call.
She complained of the service, the dirt and the
    crowd,
The trains were too dusty, their engines too loud.

Managers, Unions, Heads of the State
Could cope with the Press, but not with Aunt Kate.
They promised her Jaguars, planes or a bike
To arrest the threat of a General Strike.
But she being averse to both pedals and flights
Stood with her ticket demanding her rights,

Until they came up with a masterful plan
For delivering Auntie to her Cousin Anne,
'If you'll drive the train it will all be all right,
The engine so quiet not a mouse could take fright.'
So Kate drove that diesel and felt her real power,
And she sang and she whistled for one happy hour.
Her hat had blown off, and her face and her hair
Were covered in oil, but she didn't care;
And Anne when she saw her just couldn't guess
That this jolly lady, in such a great mess,
Was querulous Kate whom she'd dreaded to meet.

All you British Aunties, too painfully neat,
Learn from this solemn and serious tale,
How you too can be changed if you'll travel by
    rail.

SHIRLEY TOULSON

Stuff and nonsense

The friendly cinnamon bun

Shining in his stickiness and glistening with
    honey,
Safe among his sisters and his brothers on a
    tray,
With raisin eyes that looked at me as I put down
    my money,
There smiled a friendly cinnamon bun, and
    this I heard him say:

'It's a lovely, lovely morning, and the world's a
    lovely place;
I know it's going to be a lovely day.
I know we're going to be good friends; I like
    your honest face;
Together we might go a long, long way.'

The baker's girl rang up the sale, 'I'll wrap your
    bun,' said she.
'Oh no, you needn't bother,' I replied.
I smiled back at that cinnamon bun and ate
    him, one two three,
And walked out with his friendliness inside.

RUSSELL HOBAN

My owl

My little owl's the look-alike
Of Goethe the German poet.
He's stuck-up. He must know it.
He's always borrowing my bike

And crashing it, the silly coot.
He pedals full speed down steep hills
And bumps into a mouse and spills.
He doesn't give a hoot.

X. J. KENNEDY

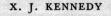

101

Special today

i

We can recommend our soups
And offer thick or thin.
One is known as *Packet*,
The other known as *Tin*.

ii

The flying-fish makes a very fine dish;
As good as plaice or skate
When sizzled in fat; but be certain that
You tether it to your plate.

iii

Now this hot-dog makes an excellent snack;
Our sausages are best pork.
If you can't get it down, please don't send it back,
But take it for a nice brisk walk.

iv

Are you tempted by our fried fish-fingers?
The last customer to succumb
Was hard to please; he demanded
Why we couldn't provide a fish thumb.

v

Bubble-and-squeak is splendid stuff
And Chef takes endless trouble
But if you feel you'd like a change
Then try our squeak-and-bubble.

vi

Try our cabinet pudding
Or a slice of home-made cake;
We serve with each, quite free of charge,
A pill for your tummy-ache.

VERNON SCANNELL

The social mixer

Father said, 'Heh heh! I'll fix her!' —
Threw mother in the concrete mixer.

She whirled about and called, 'Come hither!'
It looked like fun. He jumped in with her.

Then in to join that dizzy dance
Jumped Auntie Bea and Uncle Anse.

In leaped my little sister Lena
And Chuckling Chuck her pet hyena.

Even Granmaw Fanshaw felt a yearning
To do some high-speed overturning.

All shouted through the motor's whine,
'Aw, come on in — the concrete's fine!'

I jumped in too and got all scrambly.
What a crazy mixed-up family.

X. J. KENNEDY

Old Mrs Thing-um-e-bob

Old Mrs Thing-um-e-bob,
Lives at you-know-where,
Dropped her what-you-may-call-it down
The well of the kitchen stair.

'Gracious me!' said Thing-um-e-bob,
'This don't look too bright.
I'll ask old Mr What's-his-name
To try and put it right.'

Along came Mr What's-his-name,
He said, 'You've broke the lot!
I'll have to see what I can do
With some of the you-know-what.'

So he gave the what-you-may-call-it a pit
And he gave it a bit of a pat,
And he put it all together again
With a little of this and that.

And he gave the what-you-may-call-it a dib
And he gave it a dab as well
When all of a sudden he heard a note
As clear as any bell.

'It's as good as new!' cried What's-his-name.
'But please remember, now,
In future Mrs Thing-um-e-bob
You'll have to go you-know-how.'

CHARLES CAUSLEY

A song of thanks

It's sensible that icicles
   Hang downward as they grow,
For I would hate to step on one
   That's buried in the snow.

It's really best that tides come in
   And then return to sea;
For if they kept on coming in,
   How wet we all would be!

I've often thought tomatoes are
   Much better red than blue,
A blue tomato is a food
   I'd certainly eschew.

It's best of all that everyone's
   So tolerant today
That I can write this sort of stuff
   And not get put away.

WILLIAM COLE

Horrible and other things

Horrible things

'What's the horriblest thing you've seen?'
Said Nell to Jean.

'Some grey-coloured, trodden-on plasticine;
On a plate, a left-over cold baked bean;
A cloakroom ticket numbered thirteen;
A slice of meat without any lean;
The smile of a spiteful fairy-tale queen;
A thing in the sea like a brown submarine;
A cheese fur-coated in brilliant green;
A bluebottle perched on a piece of sardine.
What's the horriblest thing *you've* seen?'
Said Jean to Nell.

'Your face, as you tell
Of all the horriblest things you've seen.'

ROY FULLER

Waiters

Dining with his older daughter,
Dad forgot to order water.
Daughter quickly called the waiter.
Waiter said he'd being it later.
So she waited, did the daughter,
Till the waiter brought her water.
When he poured it for her later,
Which one would you call the waiter?

MARY ANN HOBERMAN

Parents' evening

Tonight your mum and dad go off to school.
The classroom's empty.
Rabbit and gerbil sleep.
Your painting's with the others on the wall,
And all the projects you have ever done,
The long-since-finished and the just-begun,
Are ranged on desks.
Your books are in a pile.
'He gets his fractions right,' your teacher says.
Your mother reads your 'news',
Is pleased to find you've prominently listed
The sticky pudding that you liked last Tuesday.

Suppose one evening you could go along
To see how mum and dad had spent their days,
What sort of work would you find up on show?
Bus-loads of people,
Towers of coins,
Letters to fill a hundred postmen's sacks,
Hayricks of dust from offices and houses,
Plates, cakes, trains, clothes,
Stretches of motorways and bridges,
Aeroplanes and bits of ships,
Bulldozers and paperclips,
'Cellos and pneumatic drills.
A noise to make the sleepy gerbil stir.

SHIRLEY TOULSON

Morning

Feeding chickens, pollard scattered like wet sand.

— Jump down stolidly from their roost
as an old sailor jumps
with his peg-leg;
underneath half a corrugated iron tank,
open ended.

I'm stepping around the bare black ground;
wire-netting propped
with lopped poles.
Moss about, bits
of brick poking through and
bones. Rusted wrench
pressed into the ground, jaws open;
a tyrannosaurus head. Reeds.

In packing cases, one side gone, the eggs
in dry grass;
on this cold morning, they're warm, smooth:
Surprising stone

almost weightless.
Bent over;
at the side of my face
the silver, liquid paddocks; steam.
My eyes and nose are damp, I see through my
    own smoke.

Finding the eggs, dry— the colour of dry sand.

ROBERT GRAY

111

Teresa nude

Teresa bathing, glancing down, said: 'Mummy,
I wonder what it looks like in my tummy.'

The answer: pictures in a range of inks
From deepest scarlet to indifferent pinks.

— Though possibly the liver, some would deem,
Being purplish-brown, outside this colour-scheme.

And pale the bowels' wrinkled furbelows,
Packaged as neatly as a brand-new hose.

Though in the 'tummy' scarcely to be placed,
The fiery lung-trees grow up from the waist.

And a few miscellaneous parts propel
Juices and dinners through the hues of hell.

Teresa, thanks for acting as our guide
To all the beauteous sights we have inside.

Yet better we should merely show our skin,
Be made not inside out but inside in —

For how could we be ever calmly viewed
If the above were what we looked like nude?

ROY FULLER

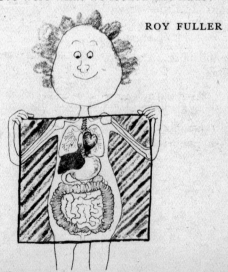

Grass

Do you ever think about grass
on the lawns you pass?
The green of it,
the sheen of it,
the after-raining clean of it
when it sparkles like glass?

Do you know what grass *is*,
those green spears showing
wherever you're going?

Every blade, to be brief,
is a *leaf*
without a twig, without a bough.
You never thought lawn mowers
went around
clipping *leaves* off the ground,
did you, now?

AILEEN FISHER

A blink

A blink, I think, is the same as a wink,
A blink is a wink that grew,
For a *wink* you blink with only one eye,
And a *blink* you wink with two!

JACQUELINE SEGAL

The tame and the wild

The fields of Farmer Hiram Brown
Are very carefully seeded down,
And all his wheat, obedient, grows
Where it was put, in tidy rows;
And no intruding bird or beast
On Farmer's velvet clover feast,
For in those pastures, rich and deep,
Graze only well-conducted sheep.

All this, with careful commonsense,
Enclosed within a sturdy fence.

Beyond the fence a mob of trees
Do exactly as they please.
The twisted banksias, yarning, lean
To tattered sheoaks, saplings green;
The tea-tree sprawls, and just for fun
The bracken, bronzing, loafs in the sun;
For crowded miles of careless land
The grey bush lounges on grey scrub sand.

And wattle-birds, shouting, squinny down
On the neat little paddocks of Farmer Brown.

DENNIS HALL

115

Bubble

I blew a bubble from my pipe
It drifted on and on —
I blew another one and thought —
'Where has the first one gone?'

JACQUELINE SEGAL

Two riddles

1

I am the shame beneath a carpet.
No one comes to sweep me off my feet.

Abandoned rooms and unread books collect me.
Sometimes I dance like particles of light.

My legions thicken on each window pane,
A gathering of dusk, perpetual gloom,

And when at last the house has fallen,
I am the cloud left hanging in the air.

2

Grand and solo, polished brightly,
Dance of practised fingers nightly,
Claire de lunar or moonlightly.

Presto, forte, pathetique,
The world is mine because I speak
A language common yet unique.

I tax to brilliant extremes
Each maestro's formalistic dreams,
All variations and all themes.

Then, when his energy withdraws
To where you sit amazed, I pause
And share with him in the applause.

JOHN MOLE

Answers 1 Dust
2 Piano

Two poems about poems

Poem on bread

The poet is about to write a poem;
He does not use a pencil or a pen.
He dips his long thin finger into jam
Or something savoury preferred by men.
This poet does not choose to write on paper;
He takes a single slice of well-baked bread
And with his jam or marmite-nibbed forefinger
He writes his verses down on that instead.
His poem is fairly short as all the best are.
When he has finished it he hopes that you
Or someone else — your brother, friend or sister—
Will read and find it marvellous and true.
If you can't read, then eat: it tastes quite good.
If you do neither, all that I can say
Is he who needs no poetry or bread
Is really in a devilish bad way.

VERNON SCANNELL

Katherine's and Jane's poem about rhyme

Dear girls, the English language, which you speak,
Is rich in meanings, but in rhymes it's weak,
So follow me from A to Z and learn
A few strange words, as forced to twist and turn
I dig up rhymes to illustrate each letter
(So just for fun let's rhyme this with Biretta,
The hat a Bishop wears, or even better,
A Turkish port, Alexandretta) —
Sometimes, alas, in order to get through
The alphabet, some assonance must do,
Like Blood and Love and Job and God, and many
More that help to turn an honest penny:
Some rhymes are rare as sunshine or quintuplets
(These pairs of lines are known to poets as
    couplets!)

We start with A — with Aniseed and Arson,
To suck in church and so upset the parson,
Or what you'd like to do when it's exam time —
Set fire to the school, but now this damn rhyme
Has beaten me, and made me swear, though
    mildly,
So let's press on to B and flutter wildly
Until we light on Basilisk and Biltong —
A stranger sight than Scotsman with his kilt on —
A monstrous reptile breathing fire and terror,
And piece of dried meat like a thong of leather.
So far my rhymes have been what we call feminine
(Like Coke and Pepsi with a slice of lemon in,
The extra bit that's left there at the end):
Rhymes when they're masculine are strong and
    send
You to the next line at a rate of knots —
For C, let's mention Comber, Cortege, Clots.
The first's a wave, the second a procession,

The third has lumps like straining milk through
    hessian —
Now, on to D, a dark and dismal letter;
Let's leave that rhyme; we did it rather better
At the start, and go to formal E,
Or should I spell it out as Formulae,
Which copes with F as well, and so to G,
Well represented here by Glossary,
A list of words whose meanings you don't know,
Like Herculean, Harpsichord and Hoe;
A task for giants, the piano's plucked forerunner,
A garden tool for weeding in the summer.
I stands for me, which modesty forbids,
And J for Jealousy of other kids;
Around the corner K delights us with
Kibosh and Kowtow — the first's a sort of myth
Of doing people down, the next's a bow
Chinese style, so low you scrape the ground.

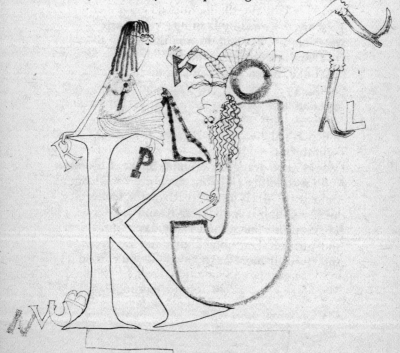

For L and M, I've picked Lese-majesty,
A two-in-one from France whose meaning may
Be treason in the legal sense, but now we
Use it of those who don't like David Bowie.
If N is Nothing, O is everything
And P is rather grand, a sort of king
Of letters, but you know the reason why —
Your Daddy's name is two Ps in a pie—
Besides, such lovely words as Persiflage
and Poet start with P — the rhyme has taken
    charge
So I look them up yourself, I'm on to Q
For Queasy, Questionnaire and Quincunx, too:
An upset stomach, then a written quiz —
Four corners and a middle, Quincunx is.
R for Rehearsal till you get it right
And S for Shambles like your rooms at night,
T is for Taciturn, the tongue-tied man
And U is Ululate, the night-owl's plan
To scare the mice by hooting; V is sharp
and Volatile, like notes upon the harp
Or Claudius, our cat, while W
Is Wonky, like a badly driven screw.
For X, Y, Z, try Xenon, Yam and Zany,
Three useless words to show that you are brainy.

And that's the end, the rhymes are rather
    cumbrous —
I could have dragged in Volta, Speke, Columbus
And lots of other chaps to show my knowledge
And earn a Merit from the Rhymers' College,
But if you find it hard, dear K and J,
Just keep this poem for a rainy day
And turn off Tony Blackburn and Ed Stewart
And try your hand at rhyming — you can do it!

PETER PORTER

Acknowledgements

The Editor and Publishers have made every effort to trace the owners of copyright and apologize to any whom they have been unable to contact. They are indebted to the following poets and publishers for permission to reproduce copyright material in this anthology:

Prudence Andrew: 'The dog' from *Allsorts 3*, Macmillan London Ltd, copyright © 1970 Prudence Andrew;

Keith Bosley: 'A house without children' from *And I Dance*, Angus & Robertson (UK) Ltd, copyright © 1972 Keith Bosley;

Charles Causley: 'Colonel Fazackerley', 'At nine of the night', 'One day at a Perranporth pet-shop', 'A fox came into my garden' and 'My mother saw a dancing bear' from *Figgie Hobbin* and *Collected Poems 1951-1975*, Macmillan London Ltd, copyright © 1970 Charles Causley;

William Cole: 'Poor Nellie' from *Cricket* magazine (as 'How sad'), copyright © 1975 William Cole, reprinted by permission of Franklin Watts Inc.; 'Simple Stan' and 'My watch' from *Allsorts 5*, Macmillan London Ltd, copyright © 1972 William Cole; 'A song of thanks' from *Allsorts 4*, Macmillan London Ltd, copyright © 1971 William Cole;

Mary Dawson: 'Late for breakfast' from *Allsorts 2*, Macmillan London Ltd, copyright © 1969 Mary Dawson;

Michael Dransfield: 'The minstrel' from *Streets of the Long Voyage*, published 1970, reprinted 1972 and 1974, by University of Queensland Press, copyright © 1974 the estate of Michael Dransfield;

D. J. Enright: 'Better be kind to them now' from *Rhyme Times Rhyme*, Chatto and Windus Ltd, copyright © 1974 D. J. Enright;

Gavin Ewart: 'The Weather' from *Allsorts 2*, Macmillan London Ltd, copyright © 1969 Gavin Ewart;

James Fenton: 'Death of a mouse', 'Animals are beasts', 'My yellow friend' and 'Squirrel' from *Allsorts 5*, Macmillan London Ltd, copyright © 1972 James Fenton;

Aileen Fisher: 'Grass' from *Cricket* magazine, copyright © 1976 Aileen Fisher;

Michael Frayn: 'When I was your age' from *Allsorts 7*, Methuen Children's Books Ltd, copyright © 1975 Michael Frayn;

John Fuller: 'How to open . . .' from *Allsorts 1*, Macmillan London Ltd, copyright © 1968 John Fuller; 'Sheep party' from *Allsorts 6*, Methuen Children's Books Ltd, copyright © 1974 John Fuller;

Roy Fuller: 'Advice to children', 'The art of the possible', 'After breakfast', 'Bringing up babies', 'Stables' tables' and 'Teresa nude' from *Seen Grandpa Lately?*, André Deutsch Ltd, copyright © 1972 Roy Fuller; 'Snow' and 'Horrible things' from *Allsorts 3*, Macmillan London Ltd, copyright © 1970 Roy Fuller;

Robert Gray: 'Morning' from *Creekwater Journal*, published 1974 by University of Queensland Press, copyright © 1974 Robert Gray;

Mary Ann Hoberman: 'Waiters' from *Cricket* magazine, copyright © 1976 Mary Ann Hoberman;

Felice Holman: 'Supermarket' and 'They're calling' from *At the top of my voice and other poems*, Charles Scribner's Sons, copyright © 1970 Felice Holman;

David Hornsby: 'Tom's bomb' from *Allsorts 6*, Methuen Children's Books Ltd, copyright © 1974 David Hornsby;

Elizabeth Jennings: 'The radio men' from *The Secret Brother*, Macmillan London Ltd, copyright © 1966 Elizabeth Jennings;

X. J. Kennedy: 'Waking up Uncle', 'Snowflake soufflé', 'My owl', 'Vulture', 'Cows', 'Who to pet and who not to', 'Mother, a dog is at the door', 'The social mixer' from *Allsorts 7*, Methuen Children's Books.Ltd, copyright © 1975 X. J. Kennedy;

Philip Larkin: 'Take one home for the kiddies' from *The Whitsun Weddings*, Faber and Faber Limited, copyright © 1964 Philip Larkin;

Brian Lee: 'What shall I do?', 'Words', 'Rain' and 'Cold Feet' from *Late Home*, Kestrel Books, copyright © 1976 Brian Lee, reprinted by permission of Penguin

Index of poets

Other Magnet Books are available at your bookshop or newsagent. In case of difficulties, orders may be sent to:

Magnet Books
Cash Sales Department
PO Box 11
Falmouth
Cornwall TR10 9EN
England

Please send cheque or postal order, no currency, for purchase price quoted and allow the following for postage and packing:

UK   40p for the first book, 18p for the second book and 13p for each additional book ordered, to a maximum charge of £1.49

BFPO & EIRE   40p for the first book, 18p for the second book plus 13p per copy for the next 7 books, thereafter 7p per book

OVERSEAS   60p for the first book plus 18p per copy for each additional book.

While every effort is made to keep prices low, it is sometimes necessary to increase prices at short notice. Magnet Books reserve the right to show new retail prices on covers which may differ from those previously advertised in the text or elsewhere.